Secrets from Yiayia's
Greek Kitchen
Meze, Soups & Dips

Written by
Sarah Pylas
and
Eva Ryan

Recipes by *Vasso Pylas*

For Zachy, Oatman and Little Teeth

Contents

Introduction 5
Our Family 6
About 7

Dips

Houmous (Chickpea Dip) Ⓥ 10
Melintzanosalata (Aubergine Dip) Ⓥ 11
Tzatziki (Cucumber & Greek Yoghurt Dip) Ⓥ 13
Taramosalata (Cod Roe Dip) 14
Skordalia (Garlic & Potato Dip) Ⓥ 17
Avocado Mousse Ⓥ 18
Special Dipping Sauce Ⓥ for Cocktail Sausages 21

Meze

Spanakopita (Spinach & Cheese Pie) Ⓥ 24
Tiropita (Cheese Pie with Puff Pastry) Ⓥ 26
Revithia (Chickpeas) Ⓥ 29
Revithia me Spanaki (Chickpeas with Spinach) Ⓥ 30
Beetroot Salad Ⓥ 32
Horiatiki Salata (Greek Salad) Ⓥ 33
Gigantes (Giant Beans) Ⓥ 34
Vegetarian Dolmades (Stuffed Vine Leaves) Served with Greek Yoghurt Ⓥ ... 36
Mushrooms Stuffed with Cream Cheese Ⓥ 39
Aubergine & Courgette Fritters Ⓥ 40
Maria's Spicy Prawns 41
Calamari Krassato (Squid in Red Wine) 42
Avocado with Prawns & Vinaigrette 43
Mackerel Savoro (Mackerel in a Sour Marinade) 45
Crepes with Fresh & Smoked Salmon 46
Bourekia (Filo Pastry Rolls Stuffed with Spiced Mince Meat) 48
Keftedakia (Small Meatballs) 50

Soups

Avgolemeno Soup with Chicken (Egg Lemon Soup with Chicken) ... 54
Chilled Avocado Soup Ⓥ 57
Fasolatha (Greek White Bean Soup) Ⓥ 58
Magiritsa (Easter Soup) 60
Hortosoupa (Vegetable Soup) Ⓥ 63
Hortosoupa me Faki (Lentil & Vegetable Soup) Ⓥ 64

Acknowledgements 67

Introduction

We are very lucky to be part of a big family that enjoys nothing more than getting together around the dining table for lots of good wholesome home cooking. Some of our happiest memories are of sharing a meal at Yiayia and Papou's, talking and laughing into the night over a glass of wine. OK, bottle...

Vasso has been feeding her family (and most of their friends) for over 40-years with traditional Greek recipes handed down to her from her mother, and her mother's mother before her.

We wanted to create this book of recipes so that our own children may also enjoy the food their parents grew up on and we very much hope that our boys will go on to pass them down to their own children too.

This is the first time that Vasso has ever revealed the secrets of her family recipes to anyone, which is both an incredible honour and quite terrifying at the same time!

Together, we took on the enormous task of collating hundreds of Vasso's recipes (all safely filed in her head), translating them, cooking them and finally photographing them!

One of the issues we encountered during this process was the way that Vasso measures out ingredients – in that she doesn't! Many of her recipes included cupfuls and wine glassfuls. However, her wine glass is just 100ml and ours is almost three times the size!

There are so many recipes that we couldn't possibly include them all in this edition; so we've focused on meze, soups and dips for now, but we hope to one day fill another book with her delicious main courses and desserts.

The stories alongside the recipes are a mixture of memories old and new and are inspired by the blog grenglish.co.uk.

Thank you so much for buying this book and we hope you enjoy cooking with it as much as we have enjoyed writing it.

Kali orexi!
Eva & Sarah

Yiayia, Eva & Sarah

Our Family

Vasso & Lefteris (Yiayia & Papou)

Panagiotis & Zachy

BB

Yiayia & Papou

All the recipes in this book belong to Yiayia and have been extensively tested by Papou for over 45 years. Now retired, they spend their days pottering around the house, watching Greek tv and still cooking enough food to feed a family of 6 for a week.

Panagiotis

Panagiotis (pronounced Pany-otti) is Yiayia's firstborn son, although he calls her Mum, obviously. Becoming a husband and father has not stopped him phoning home every day to discuss the dishes Yiayia will stock her freezer with before his next visit.

BB

Maria 'BB' was born in the middle. When she is not busy pretending to be a horse for her three young nephews, she is busy travelling the world with work or relaxing around the pool at her house in Spain.

Keri, with Otus & Leo

Angie

Philip, Kris, Alex & Uncle George

Keri

Keri is married to Eva and together they have Griwi twins Otus & Leo. He was born and grew up in Christchurch, New Zealand but has lived in the UK since 1997. He loves the Grenglish world he has married into!

The Veggie

Sarah's sister, Angie, is simply referred to throughout as 'The Veggie'.

The Syrpis Family

Uncle George and his late wife introduced Vasso and Lefteris to each other many years ago. He has a son, Philip, who also has twin Griwi boys, Kris and Alex.

About

Vasso Pylas (Yiayia)

Born in the village of Selia in Crete, Vasso moved to the UK in 1969 where she met and fell in love with Lefteris Pylas, a Greek Cypriot living in London. They have 3 children together, Panagiotis, Maria and Eva.

Vasso has worked in many restaurants over the years and also as a private caterer, devising menus based on her traditional family favourites. She is now a proud Yiayia (that's Greek for Grandmother) to her 3 delightful grandsons, who are already developing a taste for all of her wonderful dishes.

Eva Ryan (née Pylas)

Eva is the youngest daughter of Yiayia Vasso. She lives with her Kiwi husband, Keri, and their twin Griwi (Greek/Kiwi) boys, Otus and Leo (aka Leonidas, The Spartan Warrior!).

Eva is currently taking a break from her career as an Events Manager to be a full-time Mum. Writing these recipes has been a welcome distraction from the magical, if crazy, twin world.

Sarah Pylas

Sarah is a freelance writer and blogger, who started sharing stories about Greek/English family life on her award-nominated blog, Grenglish, in 2011. Since then she has written for local magazines, Red Online, BritMums, TOTS 100 and The Huffington Post.

Sarah is married to Yiayia Vasso's first born, Panagiotis (aka The Greek Godzilla) and together they have a son, Zacharias.

Houmous (page 10)

Dips

Houmous (Chickpea Dip)

There was much debate over which of Yiayia's houmous recipes to include in this book. Not only because she has many different variations, all of which are wonderful, but also because Eva's version is actually a bit nicer. Yes, we said that out loud! It is not determined whether it is the addition of lime juice in Eva's version that gives her dip the edge over Yiayia's, but we can't get enough of it.

Toasted pitta bread smothered in houmous is perfect as a snack, starter or side dish. You can also make a low-salt version with a bit less garlic for young children, although our boys much prefer it with the full 3 cloves!

V ● **Serves 8** ● **Preparation Time 10 minutes** ● **Cooking Time 0 minutes**

Ingredients

400g can of cooked chickpeas
(approx. 240g drained weight)
2 heaped tbsp tahini (sesame paste)
3 garlic cloves
juice of 1 lemon (or more, according to taste)
juice of 1 lime
3 tbsp olive oil
salt and pepper to taste
splash of water
sprig of coriander (for decoration)

Method

● Drain the chickpeas and discard the juice. Rinse the chickpeas under cold water.
● Using a food blender, combine the chickpeas, tahini, garlic, lemon and lime juice, olive oil and season with salt and pepper. See how you go, but it is likely that you will need to add a splash of water so that you achieve a creamy texture.
● Place in a smart bowl and add a sprig of coriander in the centre. Nicely served with toasted pitta bread.

For a slightly tastier version, use 80g fresh chick peas. Soak the chickpeas overnight in a bowl of warm water with 1 tsp bicarbonate of soda and 1 tbsp salt. Stir well. The following day wash the chickpeas well with cold water. Place in a saucepan and add enough cold water to cover by 3cm. Heat. When the water boils you will see a white froth develop. Scoop this up with a spoon and discard. Loosely place the lid on the saucepan and over a medium heat cook until the chickpeas are well cooked/very soft. Check on the consistency every now and then and ensure that the chickpeas are just about covered with water. You may need to add some cold water. When cooked, drain the chickpeas but keep the juice and use this liquid to achieve a creamy texture for your houmous. Note to allow the chickpeas to cool before you prepare your houmous.

Eva's tip
● *Add a chili or two to give a spicy kick to your houmous!*

Yiayia's tip
● *If you feel the consistency is too thin, you can add some dry white dough (no crusts) or white breadcrumbs.*

Melintzanosalata (Aubergine Dip)

This is how it works in Greek households - you pop round to Yiayia's house unannounced at 3am and she'll whip up a spanakopita and serve a selection of dips with toasted pitta. In Crete one summer, we all descended upon Yiayia's family in Selia on a whim and within seconds a plate of food was pushed into our hands and the Raki was opened. This is not how it works in our households - if someone knocked on our door at 3am, we would assume it was a burglar and call the police. To be taken seriously as a good Greek wife, we really need to up our game! Melintzanosalata is quick and easy to prepare, plus can be kept in the fridge for when those unexpected guests pop in.

The addition of walnuts in Yiayia's melintzanosalata goes wonderfully with chunks of warm bread, raw veggies, and salty cheeses.

Ⓥ ● Serves 8 ● Preparation Time 15 minutes ● Cooking Time 30 minutes

Ingredients

1 large aubergine
6 large garlic cloves
juice of 1½ lemons
10 walnut halves
5 tbsp olive oil
salt and pepper to taste
sprig of parsley
(for decoration)

Method

● Preheat oven to 180°C.
● Wash the aubergine well and wrap with foil so it is completely covered. Place in the oven and bake for 30 minutes.
● Remove the aubergine from the oven and allow to cool. Using a knife, cut the stalk off and remove the skin (cooking in the oven should allow easy removal of the skin).
● Cut into chunks.
● In a food blender mix the aubergine, garlic, lemon juice, walnuts, olive oil and season with salt and pepper. Mix until you have a thick cream.
● Place in a smart bowl and add a sprig of parsley in the centre.
● Nicely served with toasted pitta bread, crusty French bread or toasted wholemeal bread.

Yiayia's tip

● *Add more garlic for an even greater piccante taste! This dip is best with lots of garlic, which will make your tongue tingle!*

Tzatziki (Cucumber & Greek Yoghurt Dip)

Many a summer barbecue has been scuppered over the years because of the English weather. Not many of us are so bold as to tempt fate by even saying the word 'barbecue' out loud between the months of May to August. Not so for Yiayia. Rain has never stopped her from putting on her usual Greek feast whenever she has people over for lunch. We have often arrived on a drizzly Saturday afternoon to find Yiayia in the garden with a utensil in one hand and an umbrella to protect the white coals – not her – from the rain in the other. Accompanying the souvlaki, lamb chops, three different kinds of sausages, chicken legs, pork steaks and ribs she routinely serves to her guests, will always be this delightful (and very garlicky!) dip.

Add a big dollop of Yiayia's tzatziki to your barbecued meats and salad, or serve as a dip with raw veggies and toasted pitta bread.

Ⓥ ● **Serves 8** ● **Preparation Time 15 minutes** ● **Cooking Time 0 minutes**

Ingredients

½ large cucumber, peeled and grated
500g Greek yoghurt
2 large garlic cloves, finely grated
1 tbsp fresh mint, finely chopped
2 tbsp olive oil
1½ tbsp white wine vinegar
salt and pepper to taste
sprig of mint (for decoration)

Method

● Peel the cucumber and grate onto a large plate. Give it a good shake of salt. Using your hands squeeze out as much of the juice as you can from the cucumber (the added salt will help draw out the water). Then place on some kitchen roll and press down to ensure the remaining water is absorbed.
● Place the cucumber pulp into a bowl.
● Add the yoghurt, garlic, mint, olive oil, vinegar and season with salt and pepper. Combine gently with a fork until all ingredients are mixed well.
● Place in a smart bowl and add a sprig of mint in the centre.
● Nicely served with toasted pitta bread.

Yiayia's tip

● *If after some time you find that excess water residue has appeared round the top sides of the bowl, just absorb it using a piece of kitchen roll.*

Taramosalata (Cod Roe Dip)

Lunch at Yiayia and Papou's is always a feast, even when it is not meant to be. One day we popped in to see them on our way to visit 'The Veggie' who lives nearby. As always, Yiayia had prepared meze in case anyone felt a bit peckish. As we all sat down and chatted, a selection of dips were placed on the table in front of us, which we politely tucked into. This was all the encouragement Yiayia needed to bring out the prawns, mini cheese pies, stuffed mushrooms and courgette fritters. After consuming everything presented to us, we were now quite late. As we got up to leave, Papou turned to us all and said: "What, you are not staying for lunch?"

Yiayia's fantastic recipe for taramosalata uses fresh pink cod roe imported from Greece and is full of delicious salty creaminess. Best served with toasted pitta or a selection of raw veggies.

● **Serves 8** ● **Preparation Time 20 minutes** ● **Cooking Time 0 minutes**

Ingredients

200g white stale bread – dough only
(no crusts), cut into 2 chunks
1 slice wholemeal bread (with crust is OK)
1½ heaped tbsp tarama (salted cod roe)
¼ white medium onion or
the white part of 2 spring onions
1 garlic clove
1 tbsp fresh dill
1 tbsp red wine vinegar
pepper to taste
150ml olive oil or vegetable oil
(preferably 75ml of both)
juice of 2 lemons
sprig of parsley or an olive (for decoration)

Method

● Take the 2 chunks of white bread and wholemeal slice and soak in cold water for a few minutes. Then strongly (with all your might!) squeeze out the water to remove as much liquid as possible. Place the dough in a tea towel and press down to ensure most of the water is removed.

● Put the soaked bread, tarama, onion, garlic, dill and red wine vinegar into a food blender and season with pepper. Add the olive/vegetable oil and lemon juice slowly, a little at a time, whilst mixing, to ensure that the dip blends nicely. Mix thoroughly.

● Place in a smart bowl and add a sprig of parsley or an olive in the centre.

● Nicely served with toasted pitta bread or toasted wholemeal bread.

Yiayia's tips

● *Only use fresh tarama/cod roe bought from a Deli, otherwise it just won't taste right! You will generally find two types – white or pink. Preference would be the pink tarama to give your taramosolata its distinctive colour.*

● *If you feel the consistency is too runny, you can add some dry white dough (no crusts) or white breadcrumbs.*

● *Do not add any salt as the tarama is already very salty.*

Skordalia (Garlic & Potato Dip)

When Yiayia goes shopping, she always buys more than she needs so she can give what is left to us. It is not unusual to leave Yiayia's house with new tea towels, dish-cloths and bags of fresh tomatoes. Since we have all started protesting, she has started to slip items into our car more discreetly, so we often do not discover the 17 apples, sack of potatoes, 5 peppers, 4 oranges and an industrial pack of kitchen roll until we get home!

This traditional Greek dish is made of whipped potato and loads of garlic – and by loads, we mean a whole bulb! Perfect if you unexpectedly find yourself with a year's supply! Don't let the garlic put you off, Yiayia once used 18 cloves in one batch and we could not get enough of it. This is the most delicious dip and if it is not completely demolished by the kids before it hits the plate, you can serve it with fresh veggies and pitta. It also goes brilliantly with Yiayia's beetroot salad and traditional fish & chips. Uncle George won't eat his without it!

Ⓥ ● **Serves 8** ● **Preparation Time 15 minutes** ● **Cooking Time 10 minutes**

Ingredients

2 large potatoes (approx. 550g), chopped
juice of 2 lemons
1 whole garlic bulb
salt and pepper to taste
80ml olive oil
fresh coriander, chopped (for decoration)

Method

● Peel and boil the potatoes. While they are boiling, prepare your lemons and garlic cloves.
● Once the potatoes are cooked, drain but keep the potato juice and place to one side.
● When the potato has cooled, put this and the garlic into a food blender and season with salt and pepper. Add the olive oil and lemon juice slowly, a little at a time, whilst mixing, to ensure that the dip blends nicely. Mix thoroughly.
● Nicely served with toasted pitta bread, crudités and olives. Also compliments a beetroot salad (see page 32). Best served chilled from the fridge.

Yiayia's tips

● *This is a thick and creamy dip. However, if you feel that the consistency is a bit too thick, add some of the potato juice you kept from earlier.*
● *It is up to you how much garlic you use, but the recommended amount is an entire bulb. Use less if preferred but this dip should seriously make your tongue tingle from all the garlic!*

Avocado Mousse

Panagiotis, Maria and Eva grew up with another good Greek boy, called Philip. His family lived on the same street and although they are not biologically related, Philip is very much considered to be a brother. Panagiotis, Maria and Eva are the godparents to his twin boys; Philip is Zachy's godfather and Philip's grandmother is Maria's godmother. To confuse you even more, Philip and Eva both married people from Christchurch, New Zealand and went on to have twin Griwi (Greek/Kiwi) boys!

This avocado mousse is Philip's absolute favourite. Although, don't let the name fool you into thinking this dish is a dessert – it may be mousse like in texture, but is actually best served as a dip and smeared generously on top of toasted wholemeal bread.

Ⓥ ● **Serves 8** ● **Preparation time 25 minutes** ● **Chilling time 4-5 hours**

Ingredients

18g of gelatine
75ml boiling water
75ml cold water
2 tbsp lemon juice
1 tsp salt
pepper to taste
1 tbsp onion, grated
6 dashes Tabasco
3 ripe avocados (skinned and stoned, roughly chopped)
150ml sour cream
150g mayonnaise
2 large garlic cloves
1 tsp dill

Method

● Put the gelatine in a bowl and dissolve using the boiling water. Then stir in the cold water so the gelatine cools.
● In a food blender, combine the dissolved gelatine, lemon juice, salt, pepper, onion, Tabasco, avocado, sour cream, mayonnaise, garlic and dill.
● Turn into an 8-inch mould, ideally plastic with removable lid but any kind of non-plastic tin lined with cling film will work just as well. (Lining the container with cling film helps remove the mousse from the tin later). Chill until firm (approx. 4-5 hours, possibly longer if using a non-plastic container).
● Once chilled turn onto your serving plate and ensure you cover the avocado mousse with cling film, so that it doesn't discolour.
● Nicely presented with rocket leaves and lemon segments and served with toasted wholemeal bread.

Yiayia's tip

● To aid removing the mousse from the mould and keeping the mousse intact, place the mould in a large bowl of boiling water for a couple of seconds. This will help the mousse come away more easily from the container.

Special Dipping Sauce
for Cocktail Sausages

Every December, Panagiotis and Keri take Yiayia to France for the day. They have a nice lunch and return laden with sausages and wine, which we all polish off over Christmas. It is a tradition that has been going for many years and it is one of Panagiotis' favourite days of the year. He really looks forward to it, gets excited about where they will eat, what they will order for lunch and most of all, the selection of wines they will bring home.

Yiayia absolutely dreads it! Every year is the same, she says. They leave the house at 6am to catch the early train but get lost in the car on the way - every year, without fail. They then ultimately end up missing the early train and arrive in France too late to buy everything they intended to, resulting in a Super Marché dash, where they just bundle cases of wine and sausages into the boot of the car before rushing back so not to miss their return.

The assortment of sausages will always include mini sausages, which are best eaten by the handful! This tangy dipping sauce is the perfect accompaniment.

V ● **Serves 10** ● **Preparation Time 5 minutes** ● **Cooking Time 0 minutes**

Ingredients
200g of tomato ketchup
1 tsp Worcester sauce
1 tsp heaped English mustard
4-5 dashes Tabasco (or more!)
salt to taste
cocktail sausages of your choice, cooked

Method
- In a bowl mix the tomato ketchup, Worcester sauce, mustard, Tobasco and season with salt.
- Place in the fridge.
- Best served chilled surrounded by cooked sausages of your choice.

Yiayia's tip
- This dipping sauce also goes nicely with bourekia (see page 48) and keftedakia (see page 50).

Spanakopita (page 24)

Meze

Spanakopita (Spinach & Cheese Pie)

Every year on his birthday, Panagiotis invites a small group of family and friends to celebrate with him. One year, cousins from Athens were visiting the UK so were invited to come along to the party. Only, a few minutes before we were due to leave for the pub, there was still no sign of Panagiotis' cousins or his sister, Maria, who had been charged with escorting them to South London. Panagiotis was just beginning to fret when the doorbell finally rang. He leapt off the sofa and flung open the front door. He did not expect to be greeted with warm spanakopita, fresh out of Yiayia's oven and transported in a taxi across London on his cousins' laps - Yiayia had insisted they could not leave without it!

This recipe is bursting with green vegetables to balance out all the cheese; and is best served with a crisp green salad as a light snack, or with barbecued meats and potatoes as part of a main meal. Wash it down with a glass of wine or an ice-cold Greek beer.

ⓥ ● Serves 8 ● Preparation time 30 minutes ● Cooking time 50-60 minutes

Ingredients

250g fresh spinach
200g Greek feta cheese, crumbled
65g cheddar cheese, grated
2 medium eggs
200ml milk (semi-skimmed or full fat)
100g Greek yoghurt
3 heaped tbsp semolina
2 tbsp fresh dill, chopped
1 tbsp dried mint
salt and pepper to taste
6 tbsp olive oil
6 spring onions, chopped
1 medium leek, cut into strips, 2 inches long
1 courgette, chopped into round slices
2 tbsp margarine
plain flour for sprinkling
(but another flour is suitable)
500g puff pastry
(ensure soft and defrosted if using frozen)

Method

- Preheat oven to 220 ˚C.
- Add the spinach to a saucepan of boiling water for 30 seconds. Remove from the saucepan and squeeze out any excess water.
- In a large bowl mix together the cheeses, eggs, milk, yoghurt, semolina, dill, mint and season with salt and pepper. Put to one side.
- In a saucepan add 3 tbsp olive oil, heat and then add the spring onions and sauté.
- Add the leek and courgette to the saucepan and lightly heat with the spring onions. When they have slightly softened, add the spinach.

- Then add your cheese mix to the saucepan. On a low heat mix all the contents together until it starts to bubble, which will take 3-5 minutes. Remove from the heat and allow to cool.
- Gently melt 2 tbsp margarine with 3 tbsp olive oil and then oil a round baking tray approx. 30cm in diameter or a rectangular one approx. 30cm x 40cm.
- Sprinkle some flour on your work top surface and roll out ⅔ of your puff pastry, so it is a little larger than the base of your tray.

- Place the pastry in the tray. Ensure that the pastry lines the sides of your tray by approx. 3cm. If there is any excess pastry, cut this away with a knife and place it with your smaller piece of pastry (this is going to be used later for the topping).
- Pierce the base a few times with a fork or toothpick as this will help the pie breathe and aid cooking.
- Pour the cooled vegetable/cheese mix onto your base pastry layer and smooth over.
- Sprinkle some more flour on your work top surface (if required) and roll out your small piece of puff pastry to the size of your baking tray.
- Position this layer on top of your pie.
- Where your base and top pastry layers meet, fold over and pinch together to seal.

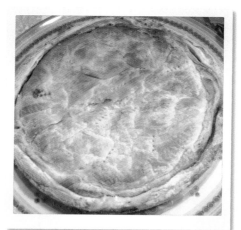

- Using a fork or toothpick, pierce the surface of your pie a few times to release steam and allow the pie to breathe and aid cooking. Lightly brush the remaining olive oil and margarine on the top of your pie.
- Cook for 15 minutes at 220 °C, then reduce the oven to 180 °C for at least a further 35 minutes. Check your pie every 10-15 minutes to ensure the top of the pie does not burn. If at any time you feel the pie is browning too quickly, loosely cover with foil. Near the end of the cooking time, you may wish to remove the foil to allow the topping to become more crispy and golden.
- Nicely served with a fresh green salad and a large glass of wine!

Yiayia's tip
- *Every oven is different! Therefore, Yiayia cannot be exact with the cooking time but it shouldn't take longer than an hour to cook.*

Tiropita (Cheese Pie with Puff Pastry)

Every year on her birthday, Eva organises a summer party in the garden and invites a big group of friends and family to help her celebrate, usually catered for by Yiayia. However, a few years ago, Yiayia and Papou were in Greece at the time of Eva's party so Yiayia had pre-prepared a spanakopita and a tiropita, which just had to be popped into the oven on the day. While Eva greeted guests and handled the barbecue, Maria and I were responsible for taking the tiropita out of the oven.

Now, for a few weeks there had been suspicions over whether Eva might be with-child. We watched as she moved around the garden, clutching a pint glass of juice and refusing offers of fizz. Our eyes followed her to the food table, where she turned her nose up at the taramosalta and held her arm protectively across her tummy. Her gaze met ours and we felt for sure that our stalking had been rumbled, but as Eva headed towards us, we caught our first whiff of it – the unmistakable aroma of tiropita burning in the oven behind us!

There are many different ways to make tiropita, depending on your preference for puff or filo pastry and types of cheese. Yiayia's version is made using puff pastry and a mix of crumbled feta and cheddar cheese to give it a bolder flavour. In Greece, tiropita is an everyday breakfast choice but it can also be enjoyed as a snack, appetiser or side dish.

(V) ● Serves 8 ● Preparation time 40 minutes ● Cooking time 45-50 minutes

Ingredients

3 medium eggs
420ml milk (semi skimmed or full fat)
400g Greek feta cheese, crumbled
200g cheddar cheese, grated
170g Greek yoghurt
1 tbsp mint, dried or fresh or mix of both
salt and pepper to taste
2 heaped tbsp self-raising flour
and extra for sprinkling
3 heaped tbsp margarine
5 tbsp olive oil
500g puff pastry (ensure soft
and defrosted if using frozen)

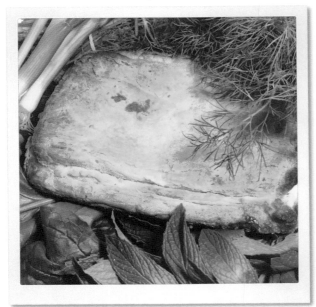

Method

● Preheat oven to 220 °C.

● In a bowl mix together the eggs, 150ml milk, cheeses, yoghurt, mint and season with salt and pepper. Mix well using a fork. Place to one side.

● To make the white sauce, firstly lightly brown the self raising flour (heating the flour first helps prevent the sauce from tasting too floury). Do this by placing the flour only in a saucepan and heat on low, stirring all the time. Just as it begins to brown, add 1 tbsp margarine, 2 tbsp olive oil and slowly add the remainder of the milk (270ml). Still over a low heat, stir until you have a creamy sauce. (You may find that there are small lumps of flour in the sauce. If need be, use a hand blender to break them up).

● Add the egg/cheese mix to the saucepan and still over a low heat, mix well with a whisk until all ingredients have been thoroughly combined. Cook thoroughly.

- Remove from the heat and allow to cool. (Do note not to add the mix to the pastry when it is hot as it will soften the pastry).

- Gently melt 2 tbsp margarine with 3 tbsp olive oil and then oil a round baking tray approx. 30cm in diameter or a rectangular one approx. 30cm x 40cm.

- Sprinkle some flour on your work top surface and roll out ⅔ of your puff pastry, so it is a little larger than the base of your tray.

- Place the pastry in the tray. Ensure that the pastry lines the sides of your tray by approx. 3cm. If there is any excess pastry, cut this away with a knife and place it with your smaller piece of pastry (this is going to be used later for the topping).

- Pierce the base a few times with a fork or toothpick as this will help the pie breathe and aid cooking.

- Pour the cooled cheese mix onto your base pastry layer and smooth over.

- Sprinkle some more flour on your work top surface (if required) and roll out your small piece of puff pastry so it is the size of your baking tray.

- Position this layer on top of your pie.

- Where your base and top pastry layers meet, fold over and pinch together to seal.

- Using a fork or toothpick pierce the surface of your pie a few times to release steam and allow the pie to breathe and aid cooking. Lightly brush the remaining olive oil and margarine on the top of your pie.

- Cook for 15 minutes at 220 °C, then reduce the oven to 180 °C for at least a further 30 minutes. Check your pie every 10-15 minutes to ensure the top of the pie does not burn. If at any time you feel the pie is browning too quickly, loosely cover with foil. Near the end of the cooking time, you may wish to remove the foil to allow the topping to become more crispy and golden.

- Nicely served with a fresh green salad and a large glass of wine!

Yiayia's tips

- *If you find that the white sauce is too runny, dissolve 1 tsp cornflour in a little milk and add this to the sauce. If it is too thick, add some more milk.*

- *Every oven is different! Therefore, Yiayia cannot be exact with the cooking time but it shouldn't take longer than 50 minutes to cook.*

Revithia (Chickpeas)

Yiayia is originally from Crete and Papou is from Cyprus. However, Panagiotis, Maria and Eva were born and raised on another big island – only Britain is a little bit colder – in a house just a few doors away from the one where their parents first met. Although they made the decision to raise their three children in London, Yiayia and Papou remain close to their families in Crete and Cyprus and visit every year.

This recipe was passed down from Great Yiayia, who lived to 105, no doubt in part from a diet including good wholesome home-cooked dishes such as this one.

The lemon and olive oil used in the original version gives this dish a classic Greek taste, while the spinach alternative – over the page – provides a super green twist.

Ⓥ ● Serves 4 ● Preparation time 15 minutes, plus overnight soaking ● Cooking time 50 minutes (approx.)

Ingredients

250g fresh chickpeas

1 tsp bicarbonate of soda

1 tbsp salt

1 medium onion, finely grated

50ml olive oil

salt and pepper to taste

1 tsp plain flour

juice of 1 large lemon, or more according to personal taste

paprika (to serve)

Method

- Soak the chickpeas overnight in a bowl of warm water with 1 tsp bicarbonate of soda and 1 tbsp salt. Stir well.
- The following day wash the chickpeas well with cold water. Place in a saucepan and add enough cold water to cover by 3cm. Bring to the boil.
- When the water boils you will see a white froth develop. Scoop this up with a spoon and discard.
- Add the grated onion to the saucepan. Loosely place the lid on the saucepan and over a medium heat cook until the chickpeas are well cooked/very soft. Check on the consistency every now and then to ensure that the chickpeas are just about covered with water. You may need to add some cold water.
- Add the olive oil and season with salt and pepper. Cook on a low heat for a further 3 minutes.
- In a cup, add 1 tsp plain flour and 2 tbsp cold water. Stir until you reach a smooth consistency. Add the lemon juice to the cup and stir well.
- Add the contents of the cup to the saucepan and stir. Over a medium heat, cook, stirring all the time. The consistency will thicken in about 1 minute. Taste and, if you like, add some more lemon juice.
- If you feel the consistency is a bit too thick, add some water.
- If you feel it is a little thin, add some more flour. Take 1 tsp plain flour and 2 tbsp cold water and stir in a cup until you reach a smooth consistency. Then add this to your revithia and stir.
- If you like, sprinkle some paprika on top. Nicely served with crusty French bread and olives.

Yiayia's tip
- *Yiayia is only happy using fresh chickpeas for this recipe as they give a much better flavour.*

Great Yiayia's tip
- *Always use a wooden spoon when stirring uncooked beans. If you use a metal spoon it will brown and harden the beans.*

Revithia me Spanaki
(Chickpeas with Spinach)

Ⓥ ● Serves 4 ● Preparation time 20 minutes, plus overnight soaking
● Cooking time 1 hour 15 minutes (approx.)

Ingredients

250g fresh chickpeas

1 tsp bicarbonate of soda

1 tbsp salt

1 medium tomato

3 tbsp olive oil

1 small onion or 2 spring onions, chopped

2 garlic cloves, chopped

1 green chili, chopped

260g fresh spinach

1 tsp tomato puree

1 tbsp fresh parsley, chopped

2 tbsp fresh dill, chopped

salt and pepper to taste

Method

● Soak the chickpeas overnight in a bowl of warm water with 1 tsp bicarbonate of soda and 1 tbsp salt. Stir well.

● The following day wash the chickpeas well with cold water. Place in a saucepan and add enough cold water to cover by 3cm. Bring to the boil.

● When the water boils you will see a white froth develop. Scoop this up with a spoon and discard.

● Loosely place the lid on the saucepan and over a medium heat cook until the chickpeas are well cooked/very soft. Check on the consistency every now and then to ensure that the chickpeas are just about covered with water. You may need to add some cold water.

● Whilst the chickpeas are cooking pop your tomato in as well for about 30 seconds. Remove the tomato from the saucepan and remove the skin with a knife. Chop and place to one side.

● Add the olive oil to another saucepan (large enough to hold all the spinach initially which will of course then wilt considerably) and heat. Sauté the onion, garlic and chili.

● Add the spinach, mix well and cook for a minute or so on a medium heat.

● Drain the chickpeas but keep the juice. Add the chickpeas to the saucepan and mix well.

● In a cup, dissolve the tomato puree with some of the chickpea juice. Add the puree and the fresh chopped tomato to the saucepan and stir well. Loosely cover and cook for 3 minutes.

● Add the parsley, dill and season with salt and pepper. Mix well.

● If you would like more sauce, add a tbsp at a time of the chickpea juice you put aside.

● If you feel the consistency is a little thin add some cornflour. Take ½ tsp of cornflour and dissolve in a cup with a little water until you reach a smooth consistency. Then add this to your revithia and stir.

● Nicely served with crusty French bread and olives, or served as a main course with rice.

Yiayia's tip
● Yiayia is only happy using fresh chickpeas for this recipe as they give a much better flavour.

Great Yiayia's tip
● Always use a wooden spoon when stirring uncooked beans. If you use a metal spoon it will brown and harden the beans.

Beetroot Salad

We always head to Crete for our summer holiday with the best intentions not to return two dress sizes bigger. However, we inevitably always fail and with so much great food we return with thighs the size of two Cretan mountains. If we had the willpower to resist the permanent aroma of yumminess emanating from Yiayia's Greek kitchen, then we would eat only this simple yet delicious beetroot salad for lunch... and not just as a starter before the main meat course.

This salad is perfect served alongside skordalia (see page 17) and barbecued meats. The addition of fresh mint presents a stunning contrast to the earthiness of the beetroot and the 2 cloves of garlic used in the dressing.

Ⓥ ● Serves 6 ● Preparation Time 10 minutes ● Cooking Time 0 minutes

Ingredients

4 large cooked beetroot or 6 medium cooked beetroot, cut into ½ cm thick wedges or slices
2 garlic cloves, grated
1 heaped tsp mint, dried or fresh or mix of both
1½ tbsp red wine vinegar
2 tbsp olive oil
1 tsp capers
1 tbsp fresh coriander, chopped
1 tbsp fresh parsley, chopped
salt and pepper to taste
sprig of mint (for decoration)

Method

- Place your beetroot into your serving bowl.
- In another bowl add the garlic, mint, vinegar, olive oil, capers, coriander, parsley and season with salt and pepper. Mix well.
- Pour the dressing over the beetroot and mix well.
- Add a sprig of mint to the centre.
- A great accompaniment served nicely with crusty French bread or pitta bread.

Horiatiki Salata (Greek Salad)

In Greece, being asked to be the Koumbara at someone's wedding is held in very high regard. One of the main responsibilities is to get the bride dressed and to the chapel on time but at Eva and Keri's wedding, Maria and I were also on red wine lip duty at the reception. Looking back at the photos, this is perhaps something we should have checked on ourselves too! This simple fresh salad was served as part of the traditional Greek wedding feast.

Traditionally, it is also enjoyed as a starter, or as one of a few smaller meze dishes that make up part of a larger meal. Best served at a leisurely pace over the course of an afternoon or evening, this salad works really well with Maria's spicy prawns (see page 41), gigantes (see page 34), keftedakia (see page 50) and calamari krassato (see page 42).

Ⓥ ● **Serves 4** ● **Preparation Time 15 minutes** ● **Cooking Time 0 minutes**

Ingredients

3 medium tomatoes on the vine, sliced
1 green pepper, deseeded and cut into rings
1 onion, cut into rings
½ cucumber, thickly sliced and cut into quarters
10 Kalamata olives
250g Greek feta cheese, cut into 4 chunks
1 tsp dried oregano
4-5 tbsp olive oil (add as much olive oil according to personal taste – great for dunking your bread!)
1 tbsp white wine vinegar
salt and pepper to taste

Method

● Put the sliced tomatoes into a bowl, then place the pepper rings on top, followed by the onion rings, cucumber chunks and then the olives.
● Top with the feta. Sprinkle the oregano over the top of the Feta and drizzle the olive oil and vinegar. Do not mix at this point.
● At the table, each guest should take their chunk of feta cheese from the salad.
● Now you should season the salad with salt and pepper and mix very well.
● Nicely served with crusty French bread.

Gigantes (Giant Beans)

The first thing Yiayia will ask when you call to say you are popping over is "What would you like to eat?". Not wanting Yiayia to spend all day in the kitchen preparing food for our visit, we once replied with "beans on toast". Of course, we should have known that Yiayia would not simply crack open a can of tinned beans and she spent the night before our visit soaking these giant beans, before marinating and simmering them on a low heat. Beans from a can will take considerably less time and trouble, but will not taste anywhere near as delicious.

This hearty Greek dish of giant beans is a firm family favourite. It can be eaten as a light lunch, served as an accompaniment to a main meal, or simply enjoyed as a meze on a lazy afternoon.

Ⓥ ● Serves 8 ● Preparation time 20 minutes, plus overnight soaking ● Cooking time 45 minutes

Ingredients

375g dried butter beans (or dried Greek gigantes beans)
1 onion, grated
2 garlic cloves, grated
1 tsp dried oregano
2 tbsp fresh parsley, chopped

1 chili (optional), chopped
1 tbsp tomato puree
½ tsp brown sugar
100ml olive oil
salt and pepper to taste

Method

● Soak the beans overnight in cold water. Ensure that the water covers the beans by 5cm.
● The following day, wash the beans well with cold water.
● Place them in a saucepan and add enough cold water to cover by 5cm. Cook over a medium heat for 45 minutes or until the beans are very soft. Check on the consistency every now and then to ensure that the beans are covered with water. You may need to add some cold water.
● Preheat the oven to 200 ˚C.
● Add the onion, garlic, oregano, parsley, chili, tomato puree, brown sugar and olive oil to the baking tray (size approx. 30cm x 25cm). Season with salt and pepper.
● Drain the beans but keep the juice.
● Add a large ladle of bean juice to the baking tray and mix all the ingredients well. Place in the oven for 15 minutes so the onion and garlic soften.
● Add the giant beans to the baking tray and mix well. Taste the sauce and add further salt if necessary.
● Use your ladle to add the bean juice to the baking tray until it just about covers the contents. (Do not discard the remaining bean juice yet, as you may need to add some more later).
● Place the uncovered baking tray in the oven and cook for 30 minutes.
● The beans should be ready once a golden glaze has developed and the sauce has thickened. If still a little runny, you can lightly cover with foil and continue to cook for a few more minutes as required. If you feel that the beans have dried a bit too much, then add some more bean juice that you put aside.
● Nicely served with olives, feta cheese, green salad and crusty French bread.

Yiayia's tip
● *Yiayia believes you can't beat Greek gigantes beans so bring some back with you on your next trip to Greece!*

Great Yiayia's tip
● *Always use a wooden spoon when stirring uncooked beans. If you use a metal spoon it will brown and harden the beans.*

Vegetarian Dolmades
(Stuffed Vine Leaves) Served with Greek Yoghurt

It is no secret that one of the most common ingredients for many traditional Greek dishes is meat. Everything else is considered an accompaniment. Yiayia will spend a lot of time preparing her menu ahead of a family meal, but should a vegetarian be invited, she will fret for days about what to feed them for lunch.

The first time 'The Veggie' joined us for Greek Easter, Yiayia called to talk about what she should cook. We reassured her that any veggie would be fine with spanakopita, dolmades, pitta and dips, plus Yiayia's legendary lemon potatoes; but Yiayia was worried her vegetarian guest would still go hungry. Finally, after much deliberation she proudly exclaimed "I know! She can eat sausages!"

These vegetarian dolmades are perfect for non-meat eaters and unlike sausages do not actually contain meat. Fresh herbs and rice are stuffed into soft vine leaves and served at room temperature with a simple squeeze of lemon juice or a good dollop of Greek yoghurt. Don't be put off by the rolling and folding technique of the leaves. After a few goes you will get the hang of it!

Ⓥ ● Serves 6-8 ● Preparation time 40 minutes ● Cooking time 40 minutes

Ingredients

2 large white onions, grated

4 spring onions, finely chopped

2 heaped tbsp fresh dill, chopped

2 heaped tbsp fresh parsley, chopped

1 heaped tsp dried oregano

1½ tsp fresh mint

50ml olive oil

juice of 1½ large lemons

250g white long grain rice

salt and pepper to taste

30 vine leaves

350ml cold water

500g Greek yoghurt

Method

- Add the grated onion to a saucepan. Cover with boiling water and cook for 2 minutes. This will remove the strong smell of onion.
- Strain the onion and place in a large bowl.
- Add the spring onion, dill, parsley, oregano, mint, olive oil, lemon juice and rice. Season with salt and pepper. Mix well.
- If you are using fresh vine leaves, boil some water in a saucepan. Then remove the saucepan from the heat and add the fresh vine leaves for 3 minutes so that they soften and are more malleable.
- Remove the vine leaves from the water by draining in a colander, being careful to keep the leaves intact.
- Lightly oil a small saucepan and place two or three torn vine leaves flat on the bottom (this should help prevent the dolmades from burning).

- Take a vine leaf and flatten on your work surface, ensuring that the rough side is face up and the shiny side is face down, with the stalk of the leaf facing you.
- Take a tsp of the rice mix and place in the bottom centre of the leaf. Wrap and roll the leaf quite tightly, tucking the sides in as you go. You may need to make a judgment call on larger leaves, in that you may have to cut them a bit smaller, so the dolma is not too leafy.

- Place the roll in the small saucepan seam-side down.
- Continue this process placing the rolls closely together and neatly in layers.
- Place a small saucer on top of the stuffed vine leaves in the saucepan (this will ensure that whilst they are cooking they do not boil and overspill).
- Add 350ml cold water and then place the lid on the saucepan.
- Over a very low heat, cook the vine leaves for 40 minutes. However, do keep an eye on the dolmades whilst cooking as you do not want them to dry out. Add some more water if required.
- Remove from the heat and allow to cool (approx. 1 hour).
- Remove the dolmades from the saucepan and place in your serving bowl.
- Serve with a good dollop of Greek yoghurt.

Yiayia's tip
- *Ideally use vine leaves grown in your own garden! They'll be much tastier!*

Mushrooms Stuffed with Cream Cheese

Most of the family are a big fan of mushrooms, however Panagiotis and Zachy are not so keen. Usually, we have to cut them up into small pieces and hide them in sauces and casseroles. In their whole form, Panagiotis will pick them out and push them to the side of his plate, whereas Zachy will probably turn his nose up and refuse to eat anything at all. However, slap a bit of cream cheese on top of a mushroom and they'll fight over the last one!

These stuffed mushrooms are really moorish and great for parties. They can also be enjoyed as a snack, starter, or just because you can't resist another...

Ⓥ ● Serves 4-8 ● Preparation time 20 minutes ● Cooking time 10 minutes

Ingredients

16 chestnut mushrooms
180g cream cheese (light version if preferred)
1 garlic clove, finely grated
salt and pepper to taste

1 large egg
50g breadcrumbs
approx. 250ml vegetable oil

Method

● Wash your mushrooms. Place with the stalk facing down on kitchen roll and dry well.
● Twist and pull off each of the stalks from the mushroom so each mushroom is left hollow. (Stalks are not used for this recipe but put aside and find a use elsewhere). You can use a rounded knife to help remove the stalks if they do not come clean away.
● Sprinkle some salt inside each mushroom hollow.
● In a bowl add the cream cheese, garlic and season with salt and pepper. Gently mix.
● Using a rounded knife or small spatula, fill the mushroom cap with the cheese mix. Ensure you press the mix down into the mushroom, so it is stuffed as much as possible.
● Beat the egg in a bowl.
● In a separate bowl add the breadcrumbs.
● Take each individual mushroom and dip into the beaten egg, ensuring that the whole mushroom has been covered. Then place the mushroom in the bowl with the breadcrumbs and again ensure it is fully covered with breadcrumbs. Place on a tray.
● Heat the vegetable oil in a small saucepan (to hold 6 mushrooms). There should be enough oil in the saucepan to cover half the mushroom.
● Ensure the oil is extremely hot before you carefully add the mushrooms, as it is then less likely for your cheese mix to fall out whilst cooking.
● Add 4-6 mushrooms at a time. Cook the mushrooms for 30 seconds or so on each side and remove when crisp and browned.
● Once cooked, place the mushrooms on kitchen roll to absorb some of the oil.
● Place on a serving dish.
● Best served hot with a crispy outer coating and a smooth, soft centre. (If left to cool for too long, the breadcrumbs will soften).
● These mushrooms are lovely as a meze but also nicely served with salad or rice.

Yiayia's tip

● *You can add a potato wedge with the vegetable oil to the saucepan to prevent too strong an oil aroma developing.*

Aubergine & Courgette Fritters

We like to think we're pretty good at making sure we all eat enough veggies, although when presented with a meze table, it is sometimes far too tempting to overlook the carrot sticks and feast on the pitta and dips instead.

These crispy vegetable fritters make an acceptable compromise and often appear on Yiayia's table as part of a meze, but can also be served as a simple lunch. They are absolutely delicious dipped in garlicky tzatziki (see page 13) with barbecued lamb chops on the side!

Ⓥ ● **Serves 8** ● **Preparation Time 10 minutes** ● **Cooking Time 20 minutes**

Ingredients

6 heaped tbsp plain flour
125ml lager (drink whatever's left in the bottle!)
50ml milk
salt and pepper to taste
1 aubergine, ends cut, partly peeled and cut into 1cm thick round slices
1 courgette, ends cut, partly peeled and cut lengthways in ½cm thick strips
vegetable oil for frying

Method

● To make the batter, in a bowl whisk the flour, lager, milk and season with salt and pepper.
● Once you have peeled and sliced the aubergine, place the slices in a bowl of salty water for a couple of minutes as this will draw out some of the bitterness. Rinse the slices and then squeeze using kitchen roll to draw out further moisture.
● Place your aubergine and courgette slices on a tray and sprinkle some salt.
● In a deep frying pan add enough oil to cover the base by 3cm. Heat the oil.
● Dip the vegetable slices in the batter and ensure all sides are coated. When the oil is hot and using tongs, put the vegetable slices in the frying pan. So they cook nicely, ensure not to add too many slices at any one time. Allow to cook for a minute or so on each side or until they become crispy and golden. Continue until all slices have been cooked. You may need to top up the oil in your frying pan as you go.
● Once cooked, place the vegetable slices on kitchen roll to absorb some of the oil.
● Place on a serving dish and best served hot. If however you need to cook slightly earlier in the day, store in the larder/cool area, lightly covered with kitchen roll (but not for too long and not in the fridge as they will soften).

Yiayia's tips

● If you have any batter remaining and spare mushrooms in the fridge, you can cook them in the same way.
● You can add a potato wedge with the vegetable oil to the saucepan to prevent too strong an oil aroma developing.

Maria's Spicy Prawns

Put Panagiotis, Maria and Eva in a room together and they will inevitably enter into a lighthearted spirit of competition. Titles are awarded for being the best sportsperson (debatable, but definitely not Panagiotis), for bringing the nicest wine to lunch (Papou), being the best cook (Yiayia, obviously), most popular with the neighbours/postman/local cats (Eva) and who has the best taste in music (Panagiotis).

However, there is one competition where Panagiotis will never triumph and that is when Maria brings out the chilies from her garden. Maria and Eva can practically inhale a vindaloo without so much as breaking a sweat, which is more than can be said for their brother, who will valiantly attempt to take them on in the chili stakes but will no doubt be left with a fit of hiccups for the remainder of the evening.

These spicy prawns are inspired from the years Maria spent living in Tarragona, Spain, where she now also owns a home. The chilies she uses are home grown in her back garden and pack quite a punch, so be brave and add as much heat as you think you can handle!

● **Serves 4** ● **Preparation Time 15 minutes** ● **Cooking Time 5 minutes**

Ingredients

225g cooked, peeled jumbo King prawns
100ml Cognac/Brandy plus an extra splash
100ml olive oil
3 garlic cloves, grated
2-6 birds eye chilies, chopped (you choose how hot you want to go!)
3 tbsp fresh parsley, chopped
salt to taste

Method

● Place the frozen prawns in a bowl. Splash some Cognac or Brandy over the prawns (to help lose the fishy smell) and leave to defrost (as instructed on the packet). Once defrosted, rinse with cold water. Leave to one side.
● Heat the olive oil in a frying pan over a medium heat. Add the chopped garlic and chili, stir and cook for half a minute.
● Then add the prawns, stir and cook for one minute.
● Remove the frying pan from the heat and add the Cognac or Brandy. Stir well.
● Place back on a medium heat and add half the parsley and season with salt. Stir well.
● The Cognac or Brandy will evaporate and you will be left with an oily sauce.
● Place in a bowl and add the remaining chopped parsley on top.
● Best served immediately. Nicely served with toasted pitta bread.

Maria's tips

● *For an extra kick use Scotch Bonnet chilies!*
● *The sauce is really tasty so soak up with bread.*

Calamari Krassato
(Squid in Red Wine)

Eva's husband, Keri, has shown quite an interest in the Greek language. It is not the easiest of languages to master, so his efforts occasionally make Eva giggle. Of course, mistakes are to be expected, but most of Keri's errors focus around food. Instead of kalimera (good day) he has said calamari (squid) and papoutsia (shoes) is a word they always use ('get your shoes on', why are you wearing Mummy's shoes', 'shoes off' etc.) but one time, instead of papoutsia, Keri asked the boys to remove their pasticio (pasta bake). However, what has warmed and amused Eva the most is when he once answered the phone and instead of saying 'Hello ego emai' (Hello it's me) he said 'Hello avgo emai', which is 'Hello, I'm an egg!'.

This recipe is much easier to grasp than the Greek language and the way it is cooked in a rich red wine sauce offers a lovely alternative to the deep fried squid you find on many restaurant menus. You will be pleasantly surprised just how far this smooth fusion of flavours will go to stimulate your palate.

● **Serves 4** ● **Preparation Time 20 minutes** ● **Cooking Time 25 minutes**

Ingredients

500g frozen calamari (if you use fresh calamari, ensure it is fully cleaned with innards removed)

2 tbsp red wine vinegar

50ml olive oil

2 medium onions, cut into rings

2 garlic cloves, chopped

1 red chili, chopped or 3 dashes Tabasco

1 tsp tomato puree

100ml red wine

dash Worcester sauce

sprig of rosemary

bay leaf

4 peppercorns

salt to taste

1 tbsp fresh parsley, chopped (for decoration)

Method

● Defrost the calamari as per the packet instructions (if using frozen).
● Place the calamari and vinegar in a bowl and add enough cold water to cover all the calamari. Leave to stand for 3 minutes. Then drain and wash well.
● Gently heat the olive oil in a saucepan. Add the onion, garlic and chili or Tabasco and sauté.
● Then add the calamari and cook on a low heat. Loosely cover with a lid.
● Dilute the tomato puree in a glass with a little water.
● Increase the heat. Add the diluted tomato puree, red wine, Worcester sauce, rosemary, bay leaf, peppercorns and season with salt. Stir well.
● Then reduce the heat, cover the saucepan and simmer for 20 minutes.
● Keep an eye on the consistency and if it has reduced too much, add some water.
● Place in your serving bowl and sprinkle with parsley.

Avocado with Prawns
& Vinaigrette

In the Greek Orthodox Church, every day of the year has been dedicated to the memory of a Saint. If someone is named after a Saint, then there is a big celebration on his or her name day. In Greece, name days are usually more important than birthdays. Gifts are given, festive meals are prepared and glasses are raised. Panagiotis and Maria's name day is in August, Zachy's is in February, Yiayia's is on New Year's Day, Leo's is in April, and Papou and Otus have a joint celebration on the day of Lefteris in December.

However, Eva has always believed that her name does not have a specific day to call its own and has missed out on this extra special 'birthday'. Imagine our surprise when casually browsing an online name day calendar (as you do!) to find that all the other Evas in the world have actually been celebrating with the Evangelines' and the Evangelos' in March!

This light avocado dish is a very presentable part of any name day feast and is bursting with good fats and protein. It can also be enjoyed as a starter, snack or light lunch.

● **Serves 2** ● **Preparation Time 10 minutes** ● **Cooking Time 0 minutes**

Ingredients
for the vinaigrette

1 tsp Dijon mustard
½ tsp sugar
1 tbsp cider or white wine vinegar
2 tbsp olive oil
salt and pepper to taste

1 ripe avocado
12-16 cooked prawns
sprig of dill (for decoration)

Method
● To make the dressing mix the mustard, sugar, vinegar and olive oil and season with salt and pepper.
● Add the prawns to the dressing and mix well.
● Cut the avocado in half and remove the stone.
● Spoon the prawns with the vinaigrette dressing into each pit.
● Place the dill on top to serve.

Yiayia's tip
● *Add a few dashes of Tabasco to the vinaigrette sauce to give it a bit of a kick.*

Mackerel Savoro
(Mackerel in a Sour Marinade)

At home, there are two things that Panagiotis is better at cooking – big chunks of meat and whole fish on the bone. He is at his happiest in the kitchen when marinating beef for our Sunday roast, skewing pork for the barbie, or deboning fish for the griddle. Just don't expect anything to accompany it! Remembering to prepare any vegetables or side dishes is not something Panagiotis ever aspires to achieve!

Yiayia's traditional Greek Cypriot mackerel recipe is perfect for cooks who love to focus on the main attraction and keep sides on the, well, sideline! It is covered in a thick sour rosemary sauce and served cold. Just pop a bit of toasted pitta, wholemeal bread or a light green salad on the side and pour yourself a big chilled glass of white wine.

● **Serves 4** ● **Preparation Time 15 minutes** ● **Cooking Time 15 minutes**

Ingredients

4 mackerel fillets
juice of ½ lemon
2 tbsp olive oil plus extra for drizzling
salt and pepper to taste
1 heaped tsp plain flour
2 garlic cloves, grated

1 tsp rosemary, chopped
plus a sprig (for decoration)
3 tbsp red wine vinegar
1 tsp tomato puree
6 dashes Tabasco
200ml cold water

Method

● Preheat your grill on high.
● Wash your fillets and place in a bowl. Drizzle the lemon juice and 1 tbsp of olive oil over the fish and sprinkle with some salt. Mix well.
● Place the mackerel fillets skin side down on your grill rack and cook for 5-6 minutes or until browned. Turn the fillets over and cook for a further 3 minutes or when the skin has browned and has started to blister and bubble.
● Whilst the fish is still warm, remove the skin and any bones. Place the fish in a bowl and break up the flesh with a fork. Place to one side.
● Add 1 tbsp of olive oil to a frying pan and heat. Add the plain flour and stir. Add the garlic and rosemary and cook whilst stirring for a minute or so. Remove from the heat.
● Season the contents of the frying pan with salt and pepper. Add the vinegar and mix well.
● Add the tomato puree, Tabasco and water. Place back on the heat and cook through.
● Spoon the sauce over the mackerel in the bowl. Add a sprig of rosemary in the centre.
● When cooled, place in the fridge.
● Serve chilled. Nicely served with toasted pitta bread and a green side salad.

Yiayia's tip
● *Yiayia uses tweezers to remove the fish bones!*

Crepes with Fresh & Smoked Salmon

The Greeks are well-known for their philosophy, art and sculpture, literature and mythology; as well as their love of Greece, good food and family. Greek men are also thought to be very romantic. Papou tells a fantastic story about literally going weak at the knees at first sight of his wife-to-be and it makes us swoon every time. This recipe is inspired by Switzerland, which is where Yiayia was living when she first met Papou.

These crepes can be enjoyed at any time of day, but Yiayia typically serves them on a platter at parties, or as a first course when having people over for dinner. Couples may even wish to impress their loved one with a romantic breakfast of smoked salmon pancakes in bed.

- **6 Crepes - Serves 3** ● **Preparation Time 20 minutes**
- **Cooking Time 25 minutes (fresh)** ● **Cooking Time 15 minutes (smoked)**

Crepes

Ingredients

6 heaped tbsp plain flour
75ml lager (helpful in softening the pancakes - drink whatever's left in the bottle!)
1 tbsp olive oil
170ml milk
1 egg
salt to taste
oil to grease the frying pan

Method

- Place the flour, lager, olive oil, milk and egg into a bowl and season with salt. Mix using a hand blender or whisk.
- Place some greaseproof paper (which should be larger than the crepe) on a large plate.
- Take a non-stick frying pan approx. 15cm in diameter. Using some kitchen roll wipe some oil on the base of the pan (and do this each time you make a crepe). Heat the frying pan on a medium heat.
- Add 3 tbsp of the mix to the frying pan and shake the pan so that the mix covers the base. Place on the heat and cook for 1 minute either side. Turn using a spatula or by tossing.
- Once cooked, place the crepe on your greaseproof paper. Place another piece of greaseproof paper on top of this crepe (ready for the next one to sit on top).
- Cook a total of 6 crepes, placing each cooked crepe on a piece of greaseproof paper. Allow the crepes to cool and then cover the plate with cling film.
- The crepes can be used immediately or placed in a larder/cool area to use the following day, but don't place in a fridge or they will go soggy.

Fresh Salmon

Ingredients

270g fresh salmon fillet

2 tbsp mayonnaise

½ tsp Dijon mustard

½ tsp tomato puree

4 dashes Tabasco

1 tsp fresh dill, chopped

1 tsp fresh parsley, chopped

salt and pepper to taste

½ red pepper, deseeded and thinly sliced

½ ripe avocado, thinly sliced

handful rocket leaves

green leaves and lemon slices (for decoration)

Method

- Grill the fresh salmon fillet for 10 minutes, turning halfway. Once cooked allow to cool.
- In a bowl add the mayonnaise, mustard, tomato puree, Tabasco, dill, parsley and season with salt and pepper. Mix well with a spoon.
- Remove any skin and bones from the salmon fillet and flake.
- Add the salmon to the mayonnaise and mix well.
- Take one crepe and place on a plate. Add a scoop of the salmon mayonnaise mix at the bottom end of the crepe. On top, add the sliced pepper, avocado and a few rocket leaves. Roll the crepe and place on your serving plate. Decorate with green leaves and lemon slices.

Smoked Salmon

Ingredients

2 tbsp cream cheese

½ tbsp tomato puree

1 tbsp capers

1 tsp fresh dill, chopped

salt and pepper to taste

2 tbsp olive oil

juice of ½ lemon

150g smoked salmon

cucumber, 24 or so very thin round slices

lemon and cucumber slices, and dill sprigs
(for decoration)

Method

- Mix the cream cheese with the tomato puree, capers, dill and season with salt and pepper.
- In a bowl mix the olive oil and lemon juice.
- Take one crepe and paste the cheese mix on the whole surface of the crepe. Lay the smoked salmon and 3-4 cucumber slices at one end of the crepe. Drizzle some oil/lemon over the salmon and cucumber.
- Roll the crepe and place onto your serving plate. Decorate with lemon, cucumber and dill. If there is any remaining oil/lemon you can drizzle over the cucumber.

Bourekia
(Filo Pastry Rolls Stuffed with Spiced Mince Meat)

As a non-Greek/non-church-going/by-marriage-only kind of Greek person, it was an incredible honour to be asked to be a Godmother to Eva and Keri's twins. But with great power comes great responsibility and in the Greek Orthodox church it is not as simple as buying a frock, rocking up to church and posing for photographs with a cute baby. Although, Panagiotis, godfather to 4, would have you believe that it is.

Following the traditional hour-long service, there is a big party for all of the guests. Bourekia is just one of the foods served at a typical Greek Orthodox christening feast, or in fact, any gathering at all!

If you follow Yiayia's recommendation of using a mixture of pork and beef mince for the filling, it will really enhance the flavour of these cigar-shaped rolls. The combination of the minced meat wrapped in crispy filo pastry is simply wonderful.

● **Serves 6** ● **Preparation Time 40 minutes** ● **Cooking Time 45 minutes**

Ingredients

2 tbsp olive oil
½ onion, chopped
1 chili, chopped
250g pork mince or mix of pork
and beef mince
¼ tsp cumin
1 tbsp fresh parsley, chopped
salt and pepper to taste
3 tbsp water

for the sauce
2 tbsp plain flour
20g butter
150ml milk
2 heaped tbsp hard cheese such as
cheddar/parmesan, grated

for the pastry rolls
1 tbsp margarine
100ml vegetable oil
4 fresh filo pastry sheets (but have a spare or two in case a sheet tears)

Method
● Pre heat the oven to 160 ˚C.
● Heat the olive oil in a saucepan. Sauté the onion and chili until they begin to brown.
  Add the mince meat, cumin, parsley and season with salt and pepper. Stir well.
● Stir in the water.
● Cook until the water evaporates and the mix is dry. Remove from the heat and set to one side.

- Heat the plain flour in a saucepan until very slightly browned (it is best to heat the flour first as it helps prevent the sauce from tasting too floury). Add the butter, milk and cheese and stir over the heat until it thickens.

- Add the cheese sauce to the mince meat and stir well. The mix should be thick and have a creamy, porridge-like consistency. (Keep this in mind but you may feel you need to add a tbsp or 2 of water). Place to one side.

- Gently heat the margarine and the vegetable oil in a saucepan until the margarine has melted.

- Oil a large baking tray with the melted margarine/oil.

- Take 1 filo pastry sheet and cut into 3 parts widthways.

- Take 1 filo piece and brush the top with margarine/oil. Take a heaped tbsp of the mince mix and place 3cm from the bottom of the filo sheet and 2-3cm from each side. Pat down.

- Fold the bottom of the filo pastry over the mince and then fold both sides inwards. The underside that has been folded over will be dry - brush it with some margarine/oil. Fold the top end in once. Continue folding over creating a roll, brushing with margarine/oil as you go along.

- Make 12 rolls and place them in the baking tray, keeping them 3cm apart so they do not stick together when cooked.

- You can keep the rolls in the fridge covered with cling film if you plan to cook them the following day.

- Cook in the oven for 45 minutes or until golden brown.

- Best served hot straight from the oven. If however you are cooking earlier in the day, store in the larder/cool area, lightly covered with kitchen roll (not in the fridge as they will soften).

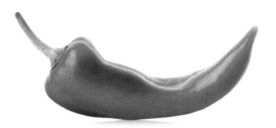

Yiayia's tips

- *During preparation keep a damp tea towel over your filo pastry sheets so that they don't dry out.*

- *The special dipping sauce on page 21 goes really nicely with bourekia.*

- *You can prepare the bourekia the previous day and keep in the fridge covered with cling film. When you come to cook, you may wish to brush some more margarine/oil over the top if you think they appear a bit dry.*

Keftedakia (Small Meatballs)

Panagiotis, Maria and Eva grew up in a very sociable household, as our own children hopefully will too. Weekends have always been a time to invite friends for a barbecue. Back in the day, before they grew older and wiser, it was also a time for the adults to crack open the Ouzo.

One afternoon after a particularly long lunch, Yiayia found Papou conked out in the shed and Uncle George passed out on Panagiotis' bed. They could not be woken for hours but when they eventually did stir, they blamed the ash from the barbecue for finding its way into their drinks and making them so ill. This recipe contains just a tablespoon of Ouzo and no barbecue ash at all!

However, don't worry if you don't have Ouzo in your liquor cabinet as red wine vinegar will work just as well. The smell of these keftedakia cooking will carry you away to a taverna on a sunny Greek island – so pour yourself a chilled glass of wine to complete the moment!

- **Serves 8 (will make 30-35 meatballs)** ● **Preparation time 25 minutes**
- **Chilling time 30 minutes** ● **Cooking time 20-30 minutes**

Ingredients

200g potato, peeled
200g pork mince
200g beef mince
200g white stale bread – dough only
(no crusts), cut into 2 chunks
2 tbsp fresh parsley, chopped
1 tsp dried mint
1 tsp dried oregano
3 garlic cloves, grated
1 medium onion, grated
1 medium egg
¾ tsp baking powder
1 tbsp olive oil
1 tbsp Ouzo or red wine vinegar
salt and pepper to taste
vegetable oil for frying or baking and to grease your hands

Method

- Grate the raw potato and then squeeze out as much moisture as you can from the shredded potato. Place the potato pulp into a large mixing bowl.
- Add both the pork and beef mince to the bowl.
- Take the 2 chunks of white bread and soak in cold water for a few minutes. Then strongly (with all your might!) squeeze out the water to remove as much liquid as possible. Place the dough in a tea towel and press down to ensure as much of the water is removed. Place the dough on top of the mince meat.

- Add the parsley, mint, oregano, garlic, onion, egg, baking powder, olive oil, Ouzo or vinegar and season with salt and pepper. Lightly grease your hands with oil or wet with water and with your hands combine the ingredients until fully mixed. Then place in the fridge for 30 minutes.
- Remove from the fridge and give your ingredients another good mix.
- Take some mince mix the size of an apricot and roll into a round or oval shape. Place onto a tray one by one.
- You can either fry or bake the meatballs.

Frying:
- Add enough oil to your frying pan so it is approx. 2 cm deep. Heat the oil well.
- Add 6 or 7 meatballs at any one time and keep rolling them over until they are brown/crisp (which should take approx. 5-6 minutes).

Baking:
- Preheat the oven to 180 °C.
- Choose a baking tray large enough to hold the keftedakia in a single layer. Add enough vegetable oil to your baking tray so it covers the base by 1cm. Heat in the oven for a few minutes until it is really hot.
- Carefully place the meatballs into the hot fat and return to the oven. Cook for 10 minutes, then turn each one over and cook for a further 10 minutes until nicely brown.

- Place in a smart serving dish and nicely served with lemon segments.

Yiayia's tips
- *If frying, you can add a potato wedge with the vegetable oil to the frying pan to prevent too strong an oil aroma developing.*
- *Keftedakia need plenty of salt and pepper! However, of course it is up to you how much you use to season.*
- *These go really nicely with the special dipping sauce (see page 21)*

Avgolemeno Soup with Chicken (page 54)

Soups

Avgolemeno Soup with Chicken
(Egg Lemon Soup with Chicken)

We all get colds from time to time, but Panagiotis seems to suffer from full-on man flu at least once a year. Coincidentally, almost always around the same time as a big sporting event is on, such as The Masters, The Ashes or the World Cup. Usually, a quick dose of fine ale is all it takes to rid him of this bug, so we are never too surprised to find him in the pub and making a swift recovery after a couple of pints.

Avgolemono soup is always offered when you've got a cold. The lemon juice provides immune-boosting vitamin C, while the chicken and rice offer comfort and nourishment when you need it most. This soup really is a big bowl of goodness that warms you from the inside out.

● **Serves 4** ● **Preparation Time 30 minutes** ● **Cooking Time 60 minutes**

Ingredients

6 pieces of chicken drumsticks and thighs
1 onion, cut into quarters
1 potato, cut into quarters
1 carrot, cut in half
1 stick of celery, cut in half
125g long grain white rice
2 eggs
juice of 3 large lemons (or more according to taste)
1 tsp cornflour
salt and pepper to taste
*fresh parsley, chopped
(for decoration)*

Method

● Remove the skin from half of the chicken pieces and then place the chicken in a saucepan. Add the onion, potato, carrot and celery with enough cold water to cover the contents by 3cm.
● Bring to the boil and then loosely place the lid and cook over a medium heat for 45 minutes. The contents should always be just about covered with water, so do check whilst cooking and if required add some cold water.
● Remove the chicken and place in a bowl. Similarly remove the vegetables but place in another bowl.
● Strain the chicken stock through a sieve incase any small bones have been deposited. Put the stock back into the saucepan.
● Cook the rice in another saucepan with water (not in the chicken stock as you don't want to use it up) until the rice is just about done.

- Add some chicken stock to the cooked vegetables in the bowl and with a hand blender mix the contents until you have quite a creamy mixture. Add this creamy sauce to the saucepan with the chicken stock. Cook over a low heat.
- Don't drain the rice, but add it and any remaining liquid to the saucepan with the chicken stock. If the rice is a bit gloopy, that's fine. Continue to cook over a low heat.
- Remove any remaining skin from the chicken and discard. Take the meat off the bone and cut into small pieces or flake using your fingers. Discard any bones and keep the meat in the bowl.
- Add the eggs, lemon juice and cornflour into a deep bowl or deep plastic container (if you use too shallow a bowl it will get messy!). With a hand blender (or you can use two forks), mix well until the mixture bubbles.
- Fill a full ladle with the hot juice from the saucepan. (Don't worry too much if you scoop up any rice.) Slowly pour this into the bowl with your egg/lemon mix and whilst pouring, combine with a hand blender at the same time.
- Fill a full ladle with cold water and slowly pour this into the bowl with your egg/lemon mix. Again as you are pouring the cold water, combine with the hand blender. (The cold water and cornflour will prevent the egg from curdling).
- With the heat still on low, slowly add the avgolemono (egg/lemon mix) to the saucepan and stir continuously. You must continue to patiently stir until the soup boils. You will however need to increase the heat slightly so you are not stirring forever! But do be careful not to put the heat on too high.
- Add the chicken pieces and season with salt and plenty of pepper. Stir and heat through. Remove from the heat.
- Ensure you taste as you go along and add extra lemon juice, salt and/or pepper according to taste.
- If you feel that the consistency is too thick, you can add some cold water, but do note that this should be a thick, hearty soup.
- Nicely served with crusty French bread.

Yiayia's tips

- *Always have extra lemon juice on offer as your guests may prefer a more tangy taste. The tangier the better!*
- *If a member of the family is feeling poorly, this is the most wonderful comfort food.*
- *If you feel the consistency is too runny, take ½ tsp of cornflour and dissolve in a little water. Add this to the soup to make it thicker.*

Chilled Avocado Soup

There can be no better auntie to our boys, than Maria. She is attentive, playful and happy to crawl around the floor pretending to be a horse. Of course, this means that they never leave her alone. As soon as she walks through the door, her nephews are climbing all over her and insisting on being thrown up in the air. This is a great distraction for us while we are trying to prepare lunch, although getting them all to the table can take forever, so fortunately this refreshing and vibrant soup is served cold.

It's perfect for summer lunches in Crete, when it is too hot to cook but you want something a bit more substantial than a salad.

Ⓥ ● Serves 4 ● Preparation Time 10 minutes ● Cooking Time 0 minutes

Ingredients

2 large ripe avocados
a few dashes Tabasco
juice of 1 lemon
200ml cold water
salt and pepper to taste
single cream or plain yoghurt (optional)
fresh mint sprigs (for decoration)

Method

- Halve each of the avocados, remove the stones and scrape out the flesh into a bowl.
- Using a hand blender combine the Tabasco, lemon juice and water with the avocado, and season with salt and pepper.
- Pour the avocado mix into your serving glasses. We use champagne saucers.
- Drizzle with the cream or yoghurt and place the mint leaves on top.

Fasolatha (Greek White Bean Soup)

It has been commented on by the family that when Eva and I get together, we do not stop talking. On a weekend trip to Spain, where Maria has a house, we did not run out of things to talk about for 48 hours. Every topic was covered from kitchen extensions to raising boys, favourite make-up brands and of course, this book. All the chit-chat drives Panagiotis, Maria and Keri absolutely bonkers, so they often busy themselves away from us to avoid it. This wholesome white bean soup takes over an hour to cook and will give you a welcome break in the kitchen, should you ever require one.

Fasolatha is often regarded as the national dish of Greece and is one of the heartiest meals on Yiayia's table. One of the main ingredients is olive oil and you will need a generous glug of it to experience this soup at its very best!

(V) ● **Serves 4-6** ● **Preparation Time 15 minutes, plus overnight soaking** ● **Cooking Time 85 minutes**

Ingredients

250g dry white beans

1 medium tomato

1 large onion, grated

2 medium carrots, chopped into 1 cm cubes

2 garlic cloves, grated

2 celery sticks, chopped

1 large potato, peeled and cut into cm cubes

1 chili, chopped

1 heaped tsp tomato puree

1 litre cold water

100ml olive oil

2 heaped tbsp fresh parsley, chopped

2 heaped tbsp fresh dill, chopped

salt and pepper to taste

Method

● Soak the dry white beans overnight in cold water. Ensure that the water covers the beans by 6cm.

● The following day, wash the white beans well with cold water.

● Place the white beans and the tomato into a saucepan. Add enough cold water so the white beans are covered by 3cm.

● Bring to the boil. Shortly after the first few bubbles, remove the tomato from the saucepan and remove the skin with a knife. Grate the tomato and keep to one side. Cook the white beans for a further 3 minutes.

● Drain and wash the white beans well under cold water.

● Clean your saucepan and put the beans back in. Add the tomato, onion, carrots, garlic, celery, potato, chili, tomato puree and water to the saucepan with the beans. Stir well.

● Bring to the boil and then cook on a medium heat for about an hour or when the beans are soft/cooked. You will notice the white beans opening when they are cooked. However, do keep an eye on the fasolatha as you may need to add some more water.

● Add the olive oil, parsley, dill and season with salt and pepper. Stir well and cook for a further 10 minutes.

● Nicely served with Greek olives and crusty French bread.

Yiayia's tip
● *If you feel the consistency of the soup is too runny, take out some of the potato cubes, mash them up and return them to the soup. This will thicken it. If you find the soup is too thick you can add a little cold water.*

Great Yiayia's tip
● *Always use a wooden spoon when stirring uncooked beans. If you use a metal spoon it will brown and harden the beans.*

Magiritsa (Easter Soup)

Greek Easter always starts the same. Yiayia will have been marinating meat, baking cakes and pies, preparing salads and re-arranging the garden furniture since 6am. A whole lamb will be roasting on a spit in the garden, or cut up into smaller souvla pieces on the barbie. Red, blue and green painted eggs will be tapped together and the holder of the last uncracked egg will be considered lucky for the next year. Everybody will shout across to each other in Greek. They will be saying things like "pass the tzatziki" or "more red wine anyone?", but you could be forgiven for thinking that Maria had just backed into Yiayia's car. We will then set up the speakers and eventually everyone will start dancing round the garden to Young Hearts Run Free.

This Easter soup is traditionally eaten to break the fast of the Greek Orthodox Lent, the 40 days before Easter. In Greece, they will use all the leftover parts of the lamb including offal and intestines, so that nothing goes to waste. However, Yiayia's version accommodates less adventurous diners as she uses only lamb's neck and liver. Her recipe is still the same in essence though and gives an authentic flavour of Greece.

● **Serves 6-8** ● **Preparation Time 30 minutes** ● **Cooking Time 2 hours**

Ingredients

4 pieces of lamb's neck
500g lamb's liver
1 onion, whole
1 tbsp margarine
2 tbsp olive oil
salt and pepper to taste
1 bunch of spring onions, finely chopped
2 baby gem lettuce, finely chopped
125g long grain white rice
2 eggs
2 large juicy lemons (you need at least 120ml juice)
1 tsp cornflour
3 tbsp fresh dill, chopped
1 tbsp fresh mint, chopped

Method

● Place the lamb's neck and liver in a saucepan and add enough water to cover the meat. Bring to the boil and cook for a further minute. Drain and wash the lamb and liver with cold water, and place to one side.

● Clean the saucepan and just place back the lamb (not the liver) with the whole onion. Add enough cold water to cover the lamb by 1cm. Loosely place the lid (so it does not overflow), bring to the boil and then lower the heat to medium and cook. Cook until the lamb is done/very soft (the meat should fall off the bone), which will take at least 1½ hours. The contents should always be covered with water by 1cm, so do check whilst cooking and if required add some cold water.

● Whilst the lamb is cooking, prepare the cooled liver. Cut the liver (with a very sharp knife) into small chunks (approx. ½cm cubes).

● In a frying pan heat 1 tbsp margarine and 2 tbsp olive oil. Sauté the liver (approx. 5 minutes) and season with salt and pepper.

- Over a medium heat, firstly add the spring onions to the liver and mix well. Then add the lettuce and mix well. (Adding the spring onion before the lettuce will help the liver absorb the onion flavour). Fry the contents for a minute or so. Remove from the heat and cover.

- When the lamb has cooked, remove it from the water with a fork and when cool enough, discard any bones and cut the meat/flake using your fingers into small (1cm) pieces. Place the meat into a bowl.

- Strain the broth (to remove any unwanted segments) into a large saucepan and keep to one side.

- Cook the rice in another saucepan with water (not in the broth as you don't want to use it up) until the rice is just about done. At this point heat the broth over a medium heat.

- Add the lamb and the liver, spring onions and lettuce to the saucepan containing the broth.

- Don't drain the rice, but add it and any remaining liquid to the saucepan with the broth (with meat, onions & lettuce). If the rice is a bit gloopy, that's fine. Mix well. Bring to the boil and then lower the heat to medium.

- Add the eggs, lemon juice and cornflour into a deep bowl or deep plastic container (if you use too shallow a bowl it will get messy!). With a hand blender (or you can use two forks), mix well until the mixture bubbles.

- Fill a full ladle with the hot juice from the saucepan (with the meat, onions, lettuce and rice and don't worry too much if you scoop up any of the contents). Slowly pour this into the bowl with your egg/lemon mix and whilst pouring, combine with a hand blender at the same time.

- Fill a full ladle with cold water and slowly pour this into the bowl with your egg/lemon mix. Again as you are pouring the cold water, combine with the hand blender. (The cold water and cornflour will prevent the egg from curdling).

- Turn the heat to low and slowly add the contents of the bowl to the saucepan and stir continuously. Add the dill and mint. Continue to patiently stir until the soup boils. You will however need to increase the heat slightly so you are not stirring forever! But do be careful not to put the heat on too high.

- Ensure you taste as you go along and add extra lemon juice, salt and/or pepper according to taste.

- If you feel that the consistency is too thick, you can add some cold water, but do note that this should be a fairly thick soup.

- Nicely served with crusty French bread.

Yiayia's tips

- *Make sure with this recipe you have all the ingredients prepared as it will make life a lot easier.*
- *Always have extra lemon juice on offer as your guests may prefer a more tangy taste. The tangier the better!*
- *Salt will help enhance the lemon flavour.*

Hortosoupa (Vegetable Soup)

Eva and Keri's twin boys, Otus and Leo, have always had a very healthy appetite. Living so close to Yiayia, means they are growing up on traditional Greek cuisine and shun other popular kids favourites such as sausages and pizza in favour of beans, lentils, barbecued meats and soups. The more vegetables you throw into this soup, the better, especially if you have invited Otus and Leo over for lunch as they will devour the whole lot!

The addition of lettuce in this recipe is not an error! The idea to add Romaine lettuce was suggested to Yiayia by a friend in Switzerland and it really does boost an otherwise fairly generic vegetable soup recipe.

(V) • **Serves 4** • **Preparation Time 15 minutes** • **Cooking Time 30 minutes**

Ingredients

3 medium potatoes, roughly chopped
1 onion, roughly chopped
2 garlic cloves, roughly chopped
1 leek, roughly chopped
150g fresh spinach
2 medium carrots, roughly chopped
1 courgette, roughly chopped
1 Romaine lettuce, roughly chopped
1 medium tomato
juice of ½ lemon
juice of 1 orange
3 tbsp olive oil
salt and pepper to taste
fresh coriander, chopped (for decoration)

Method

- Place the potatoes, onion, garlic, leek, spinach, carrots, courgette, Romaine lettuce, tomato and the lemon and orange juice into a large saucepan. Add cold water so the water covers the vegetables by 3cm. Bring to the boil. Shortly after the first few bubbles, remove the tomato from the saucepan and remove the skin with a knife. Pop the peeled tomato back into the saucepan and loosely place the lid. Cook until the vegetables become fairly soft, which should take about 30 minutes.
- If you have a hand blender, combine all the ingredients extremely well in the saucepan. If not, remove the contents and mix well in a food blender and then return to the saucepan.
- Add the olive oil and season with salt and pepper. Stir well and bring to the boil.
- Ready to serve.

Yiayia's tip

- *The consistency of the soup is down to your preference. If you feel it is too thick add some water. If you feel the soup is too runny dilute 1 tsp of cornflour or 1 tsp plain flour in a little cold water. Then stir into the soup.*

Hortosoupa me Faki
(Lentil & Vegetable Soup)

As Eva and I are both at home during the day, it is fair to say that most of the family cooking falls to us. It is also fair to say that world class chefs we will never be! Since having children to feed, our skills in the kitchen have definitely improved and we both feel much more comfortable as home cooks now. Many of our conversations with Yiayia revolve around food and from this we have realised just how easy it is to put something tasty and nutritious on the table every evening. This lentil and vegetable soup recipe is one of the first of Yiayia's we attempted on our own.

It's easy to follow and very filling thanks to the generous amount of vegetables used. A good splash of red wine vinegar at the end really brings this soup to life.

V ● **Serves 6** ● **Preparation Time 20 minutes** ● **Cooking Time 40 minutes**

Ingredients

250g green lentils

1 medium tomato

3 carrots, roughly chopped

1 onion, roughly chopped

2 medium potatoes, peeled and roughly chopped

1 leek, roughly chopped

2 garlic cloves, roughly chopped

1 stick celery, roughly chopped

1 courgette, roughly chopped

1 chili, roughly chopped (optional)

1 vegetable stock cube

½ tsp tomato puree

2 bay leaves

½ tsp rosemary, finely chopped

1 tbsp parsley, roughly chopped

3 tbsp olive oil

3 tbsp red wine vinegar

salt and pepper to taste

fresh coriander, chopped (for decoration)

Method

● Place the lentils in a saucepan and add enough cold water to cover the lentils. Bring to the boil and then cook for a further minute.

● Remove from the heat, drain and wash the lentils under cold water.

● Put the lentils back into the empty saucepan. Add the tomato, carrots, onion, potatoes, leek, garlic, celery, courgette, chili, vegetable stock, tomato puree, bay leaves, rosemary and parsley. Add cold water and cover by 3cm. Bring to the boil. Shortly after the first few bubbles, remove the tomato from the saucepan and remove the skin with a knife. Pop the peeled tomato back into the saucepan and loosely place the lid. Cook until the vegetables become fairly soft, which should take about 30 minutes.

● Remove from the heat and take out and discard the bay leaves.

● If you have a hand blender, combine all the ingredients extremely well in the saucepan. If not, remove the contents and mix well in a food blender and then return to the saucepan.

● Add the olive oil, vinegar and season with salt and pepper. Bring to the boil and cook for a further 5 minutes on a medium heat.

● You may wish to sprinkle some fresh coriander on top. Nicely served with crusty French bread.

Yiayia's tips

● *It is unlikely that you will find a pebble in your lentils, but Yiayia always checks her lentils first on a tray, just in case.*

● *The consistency of the soup is down to your preference. If you feel the soup is too runny dilute 1 tsp of cornflour or 1 tsp flour in a little cold water. Then stir into the soup.*

Tiropita (page 26)

Acknowledgements

There are so many people who have helped get this book off the ground and we are truly grateful to each and every one of you.

To Lefteris, our Chief of Quality Control and official food taster. Thank you for being such a wonderful father, father-in-law and Papou to the boys. We promise to replenish your wine cupboard soon.

Panagiotis "the Greek Godzilla", for being so good humoured about many of the stories used on the blog and in this book. Thank you for all your encouragement and support while we have been pulling this together and for helping to test so many of your mum's recipes! We could not have done it without you... plus you also managed not to moan more than a few thousand times, which has to be some kind of record!

To Keri, from the word go you have embraced all things Greek and fitted perfectly within our little Greek bubble. Thank you for the support you have given in writing this book and for being a key taster in the process, although that was probably not too much of a hardship for you!

Maria ("BB"), thank you for editing this beast and for all your guidance on getting the wording and format right. We promise to talk less and listen more on the next book!

None of this would have been possible without Michelle Rochford, who is the creative genius behind this book and worked tirelessly on making it look so beautiful! Thank you for patiently accepting change after change from two complete publishing novices and for doing so with such a huge smile on your face. We definitely owe you more than one (thousand).

Thank you so much to Oliver at mrmcquitty.com for designing our company logo and for accepting payment in spanakopita.

Thanks also to everyone who took one of our draft recipes and tested them.

Special thanks to Louise Cooper at ginghamhearts.co.uk for creating many of the wonderful food scenes featured throughout. Also to Joe Short at joeshortweddingphotography.co.uk who took the lovely shot of Yiayia on the front cover and the wonderful photos of Eva's wedding.

To our boys, you were our inspiration throughout this journey! We hope you enjoy this book. It is for you. It is for your children. We hope we do these recipes enough justice to make you want to pass them down one day too.

Finally, to Yiayia Vasso. Thank you for everything. For the food you cook for us and send us home with. For every conversation we have ever had about food, and for sharing with us the secrets from your Greek kitchen.

Kali orexi!

Recipes created by Vasso Pylas and
written by Eva Ryan

Recipe introductions by Sarah Pylas

Edited by Panagiotis Pylas and Maria Pylas

Food photography © Yiayia's Kouzina Ltd

Designed by Michelle Rochford

First published in Great Britain in 2015
by Yiayia's Kouzina Ltd

For more recipes and information visit yiayiaskouzina.co.uk

 @YiayiasKouzina

facebook.com/yiayiaskouzinaltd